ALSO BY LEILA MOTTLEY

Nightcrawling

woke up no light

woke up no light

Leila Mottley

ALFRED A. KNOPF · NEW YORK · 2024

www.aaknopf.com

Knopf, Borzoi Books, and the colophon
are registered trademarks of Penguin Random House LLC.

"Fire Season" originally appeared in *The New York Times* as part of
"The Future of Poetry, in 10 Poems" on October 9, 2020.

Library of Congress Cataloging-in-Publication Data
Names: Mottley, Leila, [date] author.
Title: Woke up no light: poems / Leila Mottley.
Description: First edition. | New York: Alfred A. Knopf, 2024. |
"This is a Borzoi book."
Identifiers: LCCN 2023042968 (print) | LCCN 2023042969 (ebook) |
ISBN 9780593319710 (hardcover) | ISBN 9780593319727 (ebook)
Subjects: LCGFT: Poetry.
Classification: LCC PS3613.O8455 W65 2024 (print) |
LCC PS3613.O8455 (ebook) | DDC 811/.6—dc23/eng/20231006
LC record available at https://lccn.loc.gov/2023042968
LC ebook record available at https://lccn.loc.gov/2023042969

Jacket art by Adrienne Brown-David
Jacket design by Michael Morris

Manufactured in the United States of America
1st Printing

my grandpa waz a doughboy from carolina
the other a garveyite from lakewood
i got talked to abt the race & achievement
bout color & propriety/
nobody spoke to me about the moon

    — ntozake shange, "senses of heritage," *Nappy Edges*

Young folks were apt to be dangerous.
This unsatisfied ambition, unrewarded merit, and the
dismal prospects positioned them at war with the given.
They were reckless . . . How could they not rebel against
circumstances that made it impossible to live?

    — Saidiya Hartman, *Wayward Lives, Beautiful Experiments*

contents

a case for / against reparations · 3

girlhood

what a Black girl wants · 11

boys will be boys will be animals will be tender will be lost will be— · 14

internal monologue while being followed home from the bus · 16

secret gardens and other invisible things · 17

birthday lists through the ages · 19

raising somebody's future woman · 20

island borned · 23

on girlhood when you are a daughter · 24

when the tinder doesn't spark · 26

The Fifth Girl of Birmingham · 28

haikus to lake merritt · 31

for Oscar Grant in the new decade · 32

First Steps · 34

neighborhood

summer 2020   ·   39

winter 2020   ·   41

Crow Call   ·   43

Elijah McClain's Last Words   ·   47

all the best celebrities are perverted   ·   48

Woke   ·   50

to the bouncers who smiled at my fake ID   ·   51

Fire Season   ·   53

haikus for sunrise   ·   55

to the black boys who love me (and then turn a blind eye)   ·   56

Finna   ·   59

falsehood

On Starting Over   ·   63

ode to the black girls who never learned to braid   ·   65

A Gemini's Worst Fear Is a Solo   ·   67

Obituary for a woman who never existed   ·   69

Cellular   ·   70

Wet Nurse   ·   72

my great-grandmother's hand in the back pocket of all your jeans   ·   73

Elegy for a body that once called itself mine   ·   75

On Fried Chicken and Watermelon   ·   77

My greatest-grandmother's will · 80

Under the Tongue · 81

womanhood

wash day · 85

going in · 86

how to love a woman sailing the sky · 87

strip · 89

Waterfalling · 90

what to do when you see a Black woman cry · 92

Respect · 94

After Want by Joan Larkin · 96

For the Women I Twerk To · 98

Futurist · 100

poem for reckoning day · 101

acknowledgments · 105

woke up no light

a case for / against reparations

I.
California says they might owe us a cent or two
if we can prove the cells that make us

split myself open rib to rib so they can get
a nice look at how i've
marbled, cratered, rotted
just to howl at a California sky

the first thing i learned about the land i spawned from
was pick a poppy and the orange thrash will send you
straight to the hollows of hell,
where san quentin signed a deal with the gardener

how warped to tell a child
her sun hot dreams would render her criminal
unless she owned the soil beneath them
rust red as a tongue rubbed raw from this constant fight

St. Louis, Oklahoma, San Francisco
the country is taking bets on how many of us
believe there is a pot of gold at the end
of this death drop
how many times they have to say repair
before it is fixed

if we had named it restitution
would they still believe they could
mend a tear in the lining of an
        ozone layer
        pantleg
        uterus

the way we do when we are looking for a miracle
the way we do when we are hoping to make it
through the decade
the way we do when we are already too late

play dead / play docile / play along
stare a beast in its mouth and dare it to bite
this is the only way to know if
the country is still hungry

II.

i want a return of the vertebrae i was born without
i have contorted, bent, braced
ached like earthquake
retreated to fault line

i want an acre
for every apology never materialized in sound
if you are ready to admit the bricks you stand on,
you must also relinquish
the house you (we) built from it
the laughter you bottled behind the door
the cars you parked side by side in the garage

repair as breath
which side of the freeway do you call home
which lung do you sacrifice in the name
of justice

repair as
breast milk, three swimming pools full
per person
per day
per millennium

can you afford what we are worth
namely   Everything
the church you pray within, the glass we blew
from the last pocket of air
left in this ecosystem

tell me, when you pay us
do you wire the money through
commissary or simply slip it

under the cell door?
how do you contend with the pink of
my grandmother's mouth
the price of a roof to die beneath
the price of a funeral

III.

on the day the check comes
my brother will change the box he calls his
express order three playstations
and a steph curry clone to make his friend

my father will lose the check
behind the dresser where his favorite
t-shirt fell last winter
with all our family photos
and he will not bother asking for a new one

i will stare at it
i will sob for all that i cannot buy back:
a photo of my great-grandfather fresh off the boat
the things this family would pay to bury
where time cannot find them
the moment in seventh grade i lost faith
there was someone to call
when the men i loved most bruised me
then pressed thumb to purple

repair as mourning
as paid time off and a passport to the only island
where we are not foreign
           we are foreign everywhere.

staples to skin
soft stretch for a broken back
curtains for the terrible things
the child has already seen

how to apologize when you are not sorry:
wash on cold

bleach the color
you wish your teeth would stain
a dryer sheet to wrap your promises in
hang on the clothesline for everyone to see
bone white dress
marrow in the filter
flesh in the closed fist of a country
always repenting
let the whole neighborhood watch
you clean now
move on
re pair with your lost self

girlhood

what a Black girl wants

i am the only child
nobody bothered to ask
     what do you want to be?
when you are the scale of a mountain and
all your teeth have wobbled
and fallen down your throat

if they had asked
i would have said
     i be a boulder of obsidian
     be a winding road to the bottom of an ocean
     be the nap you wake from dizzy

     a symphony sans sound
     a fish afraid of drowning
     a lemon tree in the desert

     there is no difference between a doctor and a cowgirl
          both always herding back to life

       what would you want if no one was around to see it?
       the child sighs, a hiccup giggle
       nothing, she says. nothing at all.

tape a bandaid on my forehead and
replace it even after the scab has fallen off
i have been shadowboxing with an imaginary friend
for so long i think my friend turned real

i want a house today.   i want a chariot.
i want your eyelashes glued to my skin.

i want to cinch the hood of my sweatshirt on a dark street
          i want three days of sleep and broth delivered straight to my stomach
                    i want the volcano to erupt   just so i can quit holding my breath

if you had bothered to ask
i would have told you
          i know how this goes
          how i will stretch
          and scramble and rearrange
          how you will squeeze at my sides
          my throat, my stomach
          how i will compress and contort and
          render myself a pulse
          quicken and explode and retreat
          and you will say
          after all that
          you did
                    she had so much potential
                    she could have been
                              the comma before your last words
                              your child's favorite nanny
                              a good girl

and i would say
after all that you did
what a shame

of all the things i could have been
never once did you think
i might not want to be small

boys will be boys will be animals will be tender will be lost will be—

kneeled on hot cement
magnifying glass pressed to eye
looking to start a backyard fire
looking for a reason to burn

we pretend the house is made of stone
not wood. we pretend
we are not flammable.
it is easier to burn than to admit
you are always one match from aflame

my mother watches her son like he is always
on the edge of choking. i watch my mother
watch her son and think, one day i will
love a boy like this. one day i will
light myself up to give him
one / clean / breath.

Brother does not see us watch through the
molten of his solitude, slams the door in my face
any little sister will tell you it is lonely:
to be the last one to let go of a held hand
the first one to clean a shared room

boys will be a closed mouth unable to swallow
eyes on the pavement, waiting for heat to catch
a leaf disintegrating like our mother's cigarettes at dawn

Brother can't hear anymore. he does not tell us
until it is too late and he suffocates inside an
uncleaned room i wish we still shared

i want to know his secrets. he wants to know
if rage can set a door frame on fire

when Brother emerges from the corpse
of adolescence, he is kind again
he asks me if i am sad today
he tells me sometimes his eyes curl back
chasing his stomach, his habits

in the crisp bitter of morning, we are trapped
back in a house on fire and he insists
on finishing his video game,
still believes he can deny his way into
a closed wage gap, fair trial, sleep

boys will be peach fuzz soft and eager to howl
wishing on a silent cup of coffee, liquor, ash

i spend nights dreaming of him
little boy, hair longer than mine will ever be
shark tooth sticking out like a second tongue

back when he was small, kneeled on cement to kiss
each ant crawling by, sobbing every time
a heel stomped them dead

boys will be boys until they are a hardened mass
no longer sculptable, until they are men
still shoveling conveniences into their cavities
and hoping no one asks them to cook tonight

boys will be animals scattering from the center
of the quake, tender as a second day bruise
lost as a toothless wolf aching to bite

internal monologue while being followed home from the bus

You are not prey
        you are beauty

    He is not masturbating
           he is breathing

        A thigh is not a muscle
                it is loose skin

           A man is not a body
                    he is a warning

                    He is a warning
           not a lover

               This is your home
           not a last resort

         It is raining
   it is not a hurricane

     You are alive
you are not safe

secret gardens and other invisible things

Summer is coming and all things
inevitably bloom

the first girl to turn scarlet
is me and mine, her and hers
belly still hanging over
thrifted rainbow tights,
girl still daring to
shuffle and skip and scream

On a Tuesday in May
little girl wakes up to
areolas doubled in size
titties appeared and bouncing
like blubber
pubes growing outward
like infection
and now a body is a thing to be
tamed
taunted
trespassed

If she is the flower
moved only by wind,
they are the bees
seeking her yellow
and she is too young
to give them all her color

the third grade mothers in the PTA
discuss ballet classes, flus, divorces

training bras
the fathers say nothing at all

A daughter is a daughter until
you no longer want to know
who followed her home today

Girl tells her brother about
the bees, about the men who
swarm and threaten to sting
he says she is lying
says she should thank the bees
sometimes they make honey

It is a lonely way to bleed.

birthday lists through the ages

5. an american girl doll with squinted eyes the color of a wave's open jaw
11. a sun room to bathe in
10. math textbooks to reverse the division of this family
6,7,8,13,14. a wheelchair
13. things to roll myself in when the going gets tough
8. a bed to call my own

9. friendship bracelets and someone to give them to
12. board games for one
16. the 1998 toyota saved from the impound
17. a private lesson in how to make someone love you.

18. a cake
15. a lover
6. heavy whipping cream for the frosting i'll conjure
7. jars to put it in
20. a battery-powered reading light

there is only so much you can do in the dark

raising somebody's future woman

when daddy thinks baby girl isn't watching,
she is halfway down the hall and heading
for the door he should've locked
she hears there is a treat waiting in the car
the treat being his hand stinging
from the last time he spanked a
wounded creature, forgetting she had a name
and that name was the rasp of his throat
when he said sorry

What's for dinner, sweet thing?

this sorrow
swaddled in a nice helping of baby girl's
history report on what coretta scott would've
said if her mans bothered to ask
what was wrong
but daddy didn't read it. he'll never know.

burnt butter girl walks her dog
down the hill wishing her training bra would
keep those bruised flaps of skin
from hurting so much
finds herself chatting with a man
in a corvette / wondering what it'd take her
to get in the car
she thinks about her aching titties, so new
she checks to see if they're still there at night
and decides to run home anyway

inside the front door, daddy's on the couch
and she knows better than to interrupt

the game with something as silly as her heart
split open like a pomegranate, sitting in her hand
so she doesn't say a word, rubs shea butter
on her oh-so-throbbing chest and washes
her hands of his sweat, her stain
that walk down the hill that wasn't
supposed to kill
the softest thing inside her

daddy walks
so his baby's
future man
can run

        daddy drawls

           Girl, pick up those clothes
           Girl, give me a haircut, won't you
           Girl, itch the spot between
                  my shoulder blades i can't reach
           Girl, swallow my terror
           Girl, spit me up clean
           Girl, Girl, Girl

so some other man can sneer
        Woman. Don't you talk to me like that.
        In my house that you clean.
        In my house that you
        carried, conjured, constructed
        from the tongue tie
        your daddy never bothered to cut.

        Goddamn, why you talking so loud?
        Goddamn, why you always got something to complain about?

you, she says
you, one that i love
you, mass of skin

i stitch
and sew
and stitch.
you rewound
the clock
replaced the
batteries
restarted the
record that will
chorus our daughter's
first dance
you. it has
always begun with
you.

island borned

here, the girls ring around a fire of clay
color of sun soaked skin, tongues reaching out

tasting sobs of mothers long gone. mothers who dove into waves
wished on a sun still pulsing like these babies' sleeping lips

ashes, ashes, the girls lay upon the laps of our once dead
now called back and wonder if the ocean loves the way we gulp

we used to believe the island was forever, back before
a new flag was raised, shadow obliterating the only thing we believed in

sun. in the meadow, mangoes and brown sugar rum go down scorching
like praise. the girls weave lace and wait for hurricanes of men

i used to think one day i'd grow up and return
to sand rich in glass so clear i mistook it for salt

before the blood. but now i know better
call us what you want, we've heard worse

in the whisper of the land's flesh taking from us what was
always meant to be ours

thunder. lightning. swim.

on girlhood when you are a daughter

every cafe i've ever been to has a man.
this man is old. and black.
just one shade darker than my daddy
and his skin is peeling like a nomadic snake
terrified of being forgotten

the man wants to sit at my table.

when an old black man
wants to sit at your table,
do you run or sing?

i am neither child
nor woman
nor smiling today.

i am bold.
i want him to sit down
because this city is so lonely
when we carve ourselves
from stone and never
risk touching
in case we crumble

i want a second birth
and a baptism
that is a forgetting
of all the rules no one
taught me.

every cafe has a man
who must be

in the face of a girl
only a man.

not my daddy's cackles rippling across his skin
not the jaundice i sip with my coffee
just a man. standing there. asking for something
i cannot give.

when the tinder doesn't spark

i dream a yellow dress,
woven from your veins
> forehead a lake's still spring
> hair a halo of golden
> pretty is one step past holy
> and two steps before the grave

You're lying if you tell me you
haven't dreamt of my body,
one creamy shade of mud
You're lying if you tell me you
haven't wanted to press your face
to the dirt just for a minute

they only want us when we've
filled in all our frown lines
dug out all the flaking patches
of our melancholy
sold our divine to the first bidder
who bothered to stare and say

without that
> hair
> tooth
> skin
> smile
> *you might just be beautiful*

i dream a red carpet of a tongue
two bodies pressed close as my front teeth should be
a strut so mesmerizingly straight you wonder

if i am not a woman but a vehicle
not a girl but dice rolled   doubles if you're lucky

There was a flash somewhere around sixteen
where i fit snug in a mustard gown i sewed myself
slipped it on for a ball i was not invited to
but knew i would find an arm to lean on,
a mouth to feed from
and instead found
after all that
an itch that crept
its way
skin to stomach

You, small girl
always wanting what you cannot have
You, small girl
wishing yourself a brand new mirror that will love you
the way i do

i dream a skyscraper of a body
halfway in the clouds and mocking

After the cameras turn the other direction
the other girls wipe the tan from their cheeks
deflate like a hot air balloon in the meadow it came from

i still slope   droop   swirl
and what am i worth in the end   if i am not pretty

The Fifth Girl of Birmingham

On the day the city's left lung blew open
the girls pressed their hair
and skipped to church,
dreaming of homecomings
and periwinkle sashes

Little Sarah at the back,
two years behind and always chasing
Before soot splattered like paint
Before her cornea callused over
with scar tissue

the roof between
Alabama stars
and those five
girls fell

down.

Sarah peeks into an already occupied grave that
could have   should have   would have belonged to her
sees her sister not a baby hair out of place
sees Addie almost

smiling.

In the thick of the daydream, where sight is returned
and the child gets to unknow the hollow walk
of the last girl left in a desert of ruin,
Sarah holds Addie's hand and they are so

young.

Maybe, looking back there was a tap   a tick   a tell
but Sarah would not know, because she was laughing—
Denise raced Cynthia to the bottom of the stairs
and by the time she got there, it was already too

late.

A window should not be able to fracture
this many ways. the girls just wanted to see
through the stained glass, put
eyes to it and saw only

scarlet.

When an artery bursts:
apply pressure to the wound
hope the body knows how to clot
hope the body knows how to

forgive.

Denise's sash was undone
Addie went to tie it, placed satin in her palm
and then the sky blew open
Addie holding Denise's sash: a lifeline cut too

soon.

Sarah knows the miracle of the last shard
left to pierce and glint and bust a town open
left to splinter Sarah's right eye
and trickle through her bloodstream for

forever.

Before every heartbreak, we do silly things
like brush our teeth
and wash our hands and
pray for our mothers
to cradle us to sleep one / last / time.

A prayer seems a small thing
in the aftermath
Sarah still standing despite
every reason she should have been on the

ground.

You do not know what it means to breathe
until your left lung collapses
You do not know how a heart beats
until your pulse wheezes and

dies.

Sarah lost more than will be buried
Small girl grown big by the time she made it out
the rubble, body punctured by every color glass
in the rainbow she once

adored.

Left with a question pulled
from the ruin:
what God would gift a girl the brutality
of being the only one left

standing?

haikus to lake merritt

when i was too young,
you saved me from the chaos
of see-through water

i sat on the grass
where you watched me kiss the girl
didn't i look young?

on the red kayak,
i paddle into the bay
endlessly seasick

i taste the inside
of our big swollen city
learning how to walk

looking for my joy
i swallowed a gold penny
found in your shallows

broke a beer bottle
danced on the sweet amber glass
flew past my curfew

i try to find you
ask geese if you are lonely
they wink and say yes.

for Oscar Grant in the new decade

two hours
into the
last rotation
of a
too-long decade

baby girl
asleep
two miles
away

the fireworks
keep going
the train
engine hot
like mercy

in the
locus of
all things
color
another one
mourned
in mural
and movie
and a mother's
endless grief

boom boom
knee cap
adam's apple
the tracks

do not
forget the
bodies laid
across them

two hours
into the
last
too-long choke
spirals
like all
others in
this city

a constant
thrash
little girl
half-asleep
fireworks
still
raging

First Steps

i believe my palms
will not lie to me
the only relics of
something starbound
and clever

my preschool self knocks
on the door and explains
the communist manifesto
in simple terms: we all need
our cheerios in the morning

i visit a playground with
my dead flesh stuck in cracks
of sidewalk

the sunken garden says i
searched for fairies and found
only my pockets
my father says i searched
his face for familiar and found
only aged scabs, peeling

i wailed and spat and burrowed
looking for my lifeline
in plastic slides and
stunted trees

i wanted to find a family album
my face in evolution
decades of Oakland and parachutes
a carving of my name
a grave, a mecca

history written in my hands
someone to read my palms and
tell me i have so much life
left over, light a match, salute
conversations with a four-year-old artifact
of my bindings
searching for an atlas
i find my own hands

neighborhood

summer 2020

I.

woke up no light
sunrise violet like crime scene
like sperm in a hotel room
June is the month of horrors
duct tape no camera
woke up no brother
woke up daughter moaning
little G sees mourning
sees clocks. do you understand
what i am saying or are you
too eclipsed / too guilty / too many
names to remember so why not
blackout.

II.

woke up to a phone call
life insurance sales gone up
and Jonathan wants me to know
i can get a real good deal, no need
to pay for a crown on my back tooth
i am worth more at midnight / asleep
toothache drowned in unconscious drool
morning always the same:
ten phone calls i know i shouldn't
answer and still
i hope, amid decades of drought
i walked ten miles
to see the dentist today because
the body does not pause its throb
in the name of grief
burned through too-narrow shoes

and when i climbed into bed
flushed chemicals from my corneas
tapped on my split molar
nothing had changed.

III.

woke up bruised
laid myself next to moonflowers
in the garden
three texts
haven't talked to you in months
but you want to know i'm ok
want to know you did enough
i see gasoline instead of eyes
and you are scared i hate you
i am scared to leave the house
i am scared to stay in the house
i am scared of the moonflowers and
scared of the nasturtiums and
maybe i would be a little more ok
if they were circles and not squares
but you do not care what i think
you woke up with crumbs
in your bed
a dandelion on your pillow.

winter 2020

It's dark at 5 o'clock now. Dinner is at 6 and you are always being watched. That's the fun of it. Put gold instead of silver forks at the table and someone will always notice. Elf on the shelf, it is easier this way. No need to attend the vigil, you are mourning in your profile photo and dinner will not be late. Lamb chops tonight, let the children open their advent calendars around the table and find a chocolate face, tell them it is their responsibility to eat that chocolate slowly so the man will remember they love him. Feel grateful they are not like Dominique from the Boys & Girls Club. Dominique does not get chocolate at the dinner table. The children eat, lick the melted Nestlé from their fingers. Dessert.

You believe the race war is a pertinent issue, and by this you mean a north pole problem. Constantly shifting. My grandmother's wedding ring: always in the pictures, never on her hand. America is obsessed with the runway. See but don't touch. Rich but no money in the bank. Diverse but no black folks in the building. A phenomenon of can you see me; watch me run; watch me be nowhere and everywhere at once. Next decade, the Wikipedia rundown will say racism sprang up like a short-lived plague, killing everyone who was not strong enuf, smart enuf, suited, white-collared, pale-hearted. And then—three magazine covers, a New York Times headline, and a best-selling memoir later—it is gone. Santa Claus lives in a moving house. No, an igloo. No, a mansion made of elf shoes and magic. Nobody has been to the north pole, but everybody has seen it. In a dream state. In a memory. In a camera's third eye.

Your daughter wants Dominique to come to Christmas Eve dinner. You reluctantly agree and prepare gluten-free cornbread so she'll feel at home and when she arrives from the bus, you wish she would have dressed up a little because it is photo night and everyone else is wearing red and Dominique is in denim. An acid wash. Dominique nibbles on her ham as you ask her what it's like living on the east side and she does not understand the question so your husband asks her about her favorite subject in school and you avert your eyes when Dominique says music because that is not a subject, it is a hobby.

After dinner, the children pull out their advent calendars and it is the final day. The flaps are grand, an illustration of a gingerbread castle, and the children rip them open, remove the chocolate. It is a woman's face today, dark instead of milk, and your daughter is delighted by the bow in the woman's hair. You remind your children that they should eat slowly, be grateful, share a little with Dominique, but when your daughter turns to Dominique, ready to split the chocolate in half, Dominique's acid wash jeans are spotted in tears and you ask her what is wrong and Dominique says, *that is my mother. In the chocolate.* And your daughter, being the child you raised, offers Dominique the whole chocolate and Dominique eats it and vomits it up a moment later, all over your daughter's velvet red dress.

After the children go to bed, you write a note to Santa Claus. You apologize for feeding Dominique cornbread she didn't like and only allowing vegan butter at the table. You promise you will help out at the soup kitchen on New Year's Eve and then you ask Santa Claus if he wouldn't mind putting in a word for your husband's job promotion. You drink his milk and eat his cookies and put the letter in the mailbox. You do it not because you believe Santa Claus is real, but because the fallacy of it keeps your yin and yang in balance. You are a good woman to believe in the north pole, to keep this alive for your children. You even got Dominique a present: an advent calendar of her own.

Crow Call

One door for Alice and one for May
take a sip from the only water that
will always leave you thirsting for more. After all
we always want what we cannot have
we never have what we've always wanted

My bus is exclusively used by the element
meaning what god created when the moon
turned a blind eye
one racket of a ride home
this is where I yearn. This is where I make
my bed and fall asleep to the rhythm of
a rattled heartbeat
resembling my own

The second / tenth / hundredth
worst thing they ever did
was force us to integrate the cafeteria
I do not want to sit next to Natalie
Natalie is not my friend
Natalie does not smell like eco styler gel
and burnt plastic and she will never know
the place I call home

Don't get me wrong, I have white friends. I love
them and they leave me scalding. I love them and
we are two ends of a string pulled taut
I am always destined to
let go first
I am always
the one

left to
fall

I never go to school where I can see it from my front door
These are the traces of my father's grasping
we know better than to be with our own
we know better than to let ourselves slip
into the soft pillow of a place
that wants us back

it is a roundabout never ending
are you on the chase or is this the getaway car?
leaking an oil trail that leads the flame right back
here

Leslie on the corner watches me walk home
Sharon gardens in her front yard just to see me saunter
The bus was a hell of a reminder today:
give away your dime for safe keeping,
expect to be left with a nickel
and a bruised trust

My great grandmother was the original Rosa Parks.
Except it was Virginia and she was so much meaner
than Rosa ever dared to be
My great granny was what you would call
A motherfucker. A bitch. A python
when it came to protecting her young

The train was on the way to a school full of girls
who shared my grandmother's
mountain nose, spiteful pout
Hold hands with the mirror, this is how
you touch god

Didn't they know we always wanted to be just us?
Didn't they know the bird was only a problem
because they envied
our chokehold on love,
insisted on shooting it
straight out the sky
so they could get a taste
of our flesh, wear our feathers

I will take a dozen potholes
gunshot and backfire and no cease to this noise
over one day of feeling so alone
I will take an underfunded school
a constant push to the outskirts
of a city I was meant to inherit
over the pity of kids who reap our sorrow

The sun crackles like fire over here
the people know my name
Don't come near my solace
Don't call a neighborhood

watch meeting just to size up
a smile

This is the only place I do not have to cave
the bermuda triangle of Oakland
where no one dares come
our way. I like my people
untouchable / disappeared
I like my people
alive.

Elijah McClain's Last Words

Boy hears a noise. Noise fades in the dark, a woman's face grease shining through the night. Boy walks, his lips a cold buzz beneath the ski mask, Midori in his ear buds, staring up at a Colorado sky that could be the ocean and thinking about which star might be a planet. Boy does not receive warning. Warning is a privilege, is a countdown before the symphony begins and boy does not understand why the police do not know he is in the choir. He is good. *I have my ID right here//My name is//That's my house.* Blue suits see the house. See window pane and chipped paint front door and a dried out lawn because it is hot summer, always hot summer. Blue suit number one looks back at boy. House//boy//house//boy. Thinks they cannot belong together. Boy feels brain fog, tries to remember himself. *I'm an introvert//I'm just different//I don't eat meat.* Boy thinks maybe he should. Maybe if he ate meat, he would not be anemic and would not have worn the ski mask to keep himself warm and would not have been mistaken for the bad kind of black boy. He is not bad. He is a violinist. He listens to Midori and goes to the liquor store to get his brother iced tea. *But I don't judge people, I don't judge people who do eat meat. Forgive me. All I was trying to do was become better . . . I will do it . . . I will do anything.* The street looks less like dried cement and more like sand. Boy did not do any of the things his mother taught him would get him killed. He needs the officers to know this, know that he is a friend and the stars are still dotted in the sky like spotlights, like eyes. *You all are phenomenal. You are beautiful and I love you. You are all very strong. Teamwork makes the dream work.* Boy feels his brain turning gray. His ear buds on the sidewalk still sounding of violin. His brother at home, thirsty. Boy has no brain left to think with, only a patch of fleshy life beneath his left pec and his skull, but something in him still hopes they will see how good he is. *Oh I'm sorry. I wasn't trying to do that. I just can't breathe.* The paramedics arrive, their needle soaring to his vein to sedate him into a sleep that will never end. The last thing boy sees is a star, one in the center of a scattered loop like a dance circle, like a cypher. It is definitely a star, he thinks, it isn't too bright or intimidating or yellow. It is almost definitely a star.

all the best celebrities are perverted

funny how easy it was to drop cosby
on the hot asphalt and keep running
cosby dried up like a grape now raisin
nobody loves that shit enough to protect it
decades later
a television is still just a series of photos

miles davis plays a mean trumpet and i must admit
i still listen to flamenco sketches when the going gets
tough as his knuckles
scabbed over from his woman's cheekbone
but a man that mean must got something
he needs to puff into that brass
so my daddy puts it on the stereo and
we all name our babies after him
hoping they might be born metallic

without the masses watching
it did not take place
this is why we walk in groups
why we pass the joint around
so it touches each pair of lips
adorned in their own peachy gloss
this is why we watch the latest docuseries
about this brother or that
husband or that kiddy-lover and say
i always knew they was wrong

trey songz made an album so hymnal that one time
we ushered him into celebrity class and now
women clutch their stomachs

try to hold intestines inside their bodies
at the sight of his smirk

too short holds women down in hotel rooms just to get a taste
of his own acid but the bay got too much pride to let him go
and how do we reconcile this love? the tides only turn
after the tsunami has already devoured and there is nowhere left to run

prove you care. sever yourself from your favorite lifesource
if you believe in prayer and partition, show me
put your lips to a trumpet and play it just like miles did
but with a tender breath
so i know you're for real
spit still clinging to the inside of your mouth pipe
women still holding it together like compact ground
threatened with erosion.

Woke

If someone asks you how many hours you sleep, on average
tell them never longer than sixty-seven percent of the night spent with
the last woman you fucked. Don't put salt on your potatoes or you
are buying into the chipped pyramid that devalues a Black woman's ashy knees
As a matter of fact, don't eat potatoes at all. For Idaho. For the protest
against pesticides. Do you even know where that came from? Surely
not your grandmother's backyard. Surely not the bulge of your throat.
Now that we're on the subject of food, we consume only in credit
cards now. Withhold change and call it altruism, we cannot support a stranger's habit
even when coins are piling up in the cupholder of a Tesla manufactured
by the hands of n-words (we can't say that without the bass of the song)
goddamn, there is so much censorship these days. Free speech, yes?
The constitution is only serviceable on a sunny day
Luckily you know the weatherman. Luckily there are only so many
pairs of sunglasses you can wear before we have all forgotten
the color of your eyes. Sometimes i want to slap the smirk
off a man in the line of a Verizon service desk. No, Apple. Apple
is where the worst ones go, pull out their phones and show me a picture
of their childhood best friend and his flat top. See, i know you. See,
we are the same. A sheet of salt floating atop waters you have never
swam in. my father says he loves the ocean, back when he waded in
somewhere around the 90s but he couldn't do it again. What if it was a nude
beach now. So much is backwards these days. They is a plural and a singular
and no father can possibly remember every she that is a they
so instead they ask their children if he is a they now too and here we are
Back at the start of a merry go round. And here i am
exhausted. Drowned in two oat milk lattes before lunch.

to the bouncers who smiled at my fake ID

i know you'd never ask but yes
that is the grin of newly grown molars
fresh nose pierced with my mother's consent
chipped nail polish from the doom
of college decisions

on the day my best friend took the photo
i thought i felt my wisdom teeth crowning
i thought i saw you wink as you hollered
the way you all do
greedy for someone to play with
and by play i mean
come with me to the swings
to the prom
rake your hand through my hair
and tell me how you have never thought
me young
don't worry, no one does

i think about your mother as often
as you think about how my ass looked
in that skirt
wrinkled from eight hours at my school desk
Does she know what you are doing tonight
how you kissed me on my seventeenth birthday
right after i asked you not to
How your eyes burned red at the sight of
betrayal on my tongue

i bought my Colorado license
on a site with GOD in neon green bold
and i told them my name was

what my mother wanted to call me
back before she knew who i would be
i know if i told you this
if you had to bear my secrets
you would not touch me
because who am i to strip
you of your hands
who am i
to make you
remember
me

Fire Season

The smoke in Oakland has hands. We are inside the palm,
choking as we feed. The teargas stings my eyes open
makes me bloodshot, makes me swallow.
My street is a warzone and by warzone I mean
hunting ground. To be Black and Girl is to not only fear the slaughter
of your body, but to fear the body itself.

I watch the men cower at my face. I watch the men sneer as they grope.
I watch the men forget what has been done to them, look
at their hands and see only how easy it is to cup them over another's mouth.
I smell the coal lingering, I smell their greatest-granddaddy's master's breath
showing them how to make a fire from black girl breasts,
feel bigger than their noose.

My brother will not understand what I mean when I say I am exhausted
of having a face and I cannot distinguish smoke from teargas
from fireworks from sirens today.
We are marching down a street that preys on me.
We are marching toward the riot gear,
toward more men in blue and belts and gas masks who do not have to gulp ash
as their zip ties slice my wrists open
and they do not worry if I am too young to be this woman

Say Her Name morphs at the rally and I am trying to rerember all the syllables
all the Sandras and Rekias and girls
who don't make the headlines because they are not dead
they have just been turned inside out
their lungs a checkerboard of gray
rotting meat and the coroner does not know if it is the fires
or the trauma

Smoke swirls and this does not stop us. The fist has begun to tremor
and we cold sweat as we march now,
the megaphone repeating again and again *I can't breathe.*
What if I am choking too

They stomp on the curbs we were ravaged on and we don't have
another choice but to keep marching,
keep believing those sounds are firecrackers and not flashbangs
or give up, let the hand tighten,
let the hand around our throats.

haikus for sunrise

it is a sullen
pink world outside the city
a still raging mouth.

in the shittiest
motel room of this small town
i roll. body. plant.

find somewhere to sleep
every night. hallelujah
for my back pocket.

to the black boys who love me (and then turn a blind eye)

i keep you toasty, boy
like your mama kept you clean
after all those long days
on the playground, the football field
the locales you go to feel bigger
than you are

i see you in tinted windows
when i am looking for threats
and you think i am searching
for your crimson lips

Every day i descend
from my nightmares so i
can stare you in those worry
wrinkled eyes and say
i love you
(too, if you ever said it first)

i prayed on your mama's
hand sewn baby blankets
you would wake up

       Good morning
       Remember that time
       i carved you a scarf from the
       extra tendons in my ankles?

i beg you to be worth
defending and even when you
are not, i do it anyway

Sometimes i lie
but the truth is i can count
the white men who have wanted
me on one hand

i do not have enough
appendages in my maternal line
to count your lashing tongues
calling after me,
your sneaker-clad feet
careful to stay clean as you
follow the nape of my neck

i beg you to be worth
defending and even when you
are not, i do it anyway

Lineage of tender gums
wombs yearning for baby boy
shadowed eyelids
i ignore, dismiss, coddle my own
hoping in the fuzzy purple robe
i wore the first Christmas i was
truly afraid

i have nothing left to threaten you with.
All the black mamas in the world
have been trying for centuries,
left you ashy in the smile
your grill showing signs of rusting
on your ego
i am done

letting you betray my faith
leave me with a sewn shut mouth

before i would ever call the cops on you
before i would let someone else's hands
hold the blame of your hurting

Do you ever think of me?
At night, when you know i
walked home alone and i am
dreaming of moving to a new
kind of city that doesn't exist
Do you ever wonder if i'd like
you to ride the bus with me
and not try to come home
with me after

Finna

go to the sto
rinse these leeks with nothing but fresh squeezed juice
kiss you like i mean it
stick my hope in the same box i keep the gun
remind my nephew there is more than one way out
forget there is more than one way out

Finna

beat yo ass if you don't get out my face
throw hands
tell you how much i love you
count down from our oldest granddaddy's death day
             113, 112, 111

3, 2, 1

Finna

wish you a happy new year without
the one you thought you'd love forever
pop firecrackers until the earth perforates
slide down into the holes like a skatepark made just for us
plug my ears
plug yours too
celebrate
         one last time

before we

Finna

repent for what we're too hardened to forgive
forgive what we're too fragile to remember
remember what we've spent decades trying to forget

love you with every gulp
of this okra juice rabbit stew hearth of a pot
go to the sto
bring you back a nice glass of something
you've been wanting
      for forever

falsehood

On Starting Over

I rent an apartment where I can smell the lake
for a reminder of all the past lives
that have sunk to the bottom of this city
I open my windows just to air out the shadows of this place
Cozy up on my mattress straight from the box and
don't even feel the pea beneath the bed

On the first morning of the first day of my new life
a seagull flies through my window and
stains my carpet in bleach white feces.
The seagull knows the color of the walls
before I paint them, knows the color of the inside
of my stomach from the shine of my window glass
and remorse is a humid tornado, consuming

I am not saying I couldn't have closed the window
I'm saying I did not
and now there is a flock inside the bedroom
I thought would be the first thing I called my own
after all those years spent packed body to body
yearning for an exit

A new beginning is only as shiny
as the window shattered just
to walk through
You will always find glass in the cracks of
your floorboards, your bloodstream

I freedom fury
I whine and war and wrestle
I fold

and cut an orange picked from
a tree I pretend is mine

Reinvent yourself enough times and you won't
know whose hands wrap around your throat.
I rent an apartment and think it can erase me.
I rent a new ribcage and think it can protect me
from everything that has already ruptured.

When you find seeds inside your orange slice,
you spit them out. Not because they cannot be eaten,
but because you are craving sweet and they are bitter.
You have plans to fly across the city and there is
now a seagull by your side and what cannot kill may choke

A shattered rib
Broken glass
Regret is unholy
not unnatural
If I want my seeds back,
I will cut another orange.
You cannot reverse
You can only revise

Open the window
Let your past selves
flock at your bedside
Let the citrus absorb
and become you

ode to the black girls who never learned to braid

somebody forgot to teach me my own name
and now i wander a memorial street
and call it a mystery

i rip my lonely out at the roots
and regrow it a heavy head of bliss
i was always meant for the chameleon life
the rebellion of baby hairs
there is no gel in my cabinet
i radiate and bust all on my own
i revolve around the stain of my satin bonnet
on the white white sheets of a hotel bed
i whip my hair on the dance floor
and don't apologize for the sting

somebody forgot to show me how to treat
my kitchen like a woman shaken from a
good fuck so i cut it off and now
i regrow it the shape of a dragon tail
i heat from the furnace of my temples
i coil from the scales of my tongue

i teach my hands how to throb
in the name of a baby not yet born
i name myself in the image of a woman
always morphing
i criss-cross planets until i find one
worthy of my frizz
i sell my build up for the price of
a lifetime spent remembering what
i left in the other room
i have a nagging sense you should've

loved me like you meant it
i déjà vu we were once knotted together
inseparable as these locs trapped
in a gel cast

somebody forgot to teach me how
to worship at my own spine
so i teach myself
the curve of every vertebra
the boomerang of every ringlet
the split ending of every
hard goodbye
i make right what has wronged me
i twist myself around who i was
meant to be and
let my follicles turn silver
the way my mother did
the year she realized my hands
could not spontaneously remember
where they came from

A Gemini's Worst Fear Is a Solo

I strut in the middle of the road
in Paris because this is something heavenly
as two bronze hands intertwined
I gamble a life alone just to wallow in this patch
of sun for five more minutes

I sob every time somebody cleaves themselves
from the one they said they loved
I say if you're not soaring on the fingertips
of this desire, it's not worth the air you reign

I risk a blind eye staring at the ground
for footprints long dead
I raise a telescope to the next star I'm longing for
and forget the color of my own sun

Some call me venomous
Some call me sickly sweet

I stack transgressions on my windowsill
and color code them
I say please before I ask you
not to come to my door again

I built these hips to hold a child and
I don't care if you think I should wait
I spilled these secrets to wreck a family
assembled of needles and most days I don't regret it

Call it morbid but I write amendments to my
will on the baseboards of my bedroom
Call it overly optimistic but I don't

believe in dirt i can't eat
Contrary to all I've been told
I don't sit on a throne not customized
to the groove of my thighs
I don't kiss a woman who doesn't look
at me like I can float in any ocean
I don't throttle my fantasies
I resurrect them

Obituary for a woman who never existed

Born sometime before the leaves began to fall
October, 1886
sixteen years before her body broke
open to create something some would call a child but
Emma would call the first of her Dead
Emma had a last name when she was born
but lost it somewhere along the way.
Passed on Thanksgiving 1916, just in time for pie.

             Some say Emma was a smart girl,
             some say she was Indian (pin straight hair, children
             hoping to be a little less of what they were)
             but all would agree she was gone before
             there was much to say about her at all.

      Maybe she was her mother's child.
      Maybe she was God's favorite witch.
      Maybe she never made it off the ship at all.

      Poor thing. Ghostly. Emma is survived by
      somebody else's husband
      beloved children running north
      a plot of dirt with

      no stone, no name, no bone.

Cellular

in the machine, my father's blood is a slushy
flavored kool-aid red and rotating, his face drooped
and clinging to the plastic chair, mouth swollen
tongue stuck through teeth thin as rolled paper
waiting for me to feed him stories of his city.
i don't tell him but he is looking as old as he is
for the first time in my life
america has preyed on him six decades too long and
it is catching up, leaving him with coal black blood
and a lifeless family tree. a decade before
daddy's brother got sick, my uncle walked home
in a city where the streetlamps didn't bother
to turn on. kilpatrick preferred a manicure
and a mistress to ems equipment but the city churned
on as all cities do, separated itself into particles the way
detroit has been known to sift and split
the way black folk have survived for longer
than my daddy's blood has existed in that body
purple in the veins. gums speckled in black.
daddy and his brother always in battle
with the concept of light, fox theatre deceiving
the street into thinking those flashes are red
when they are really a paycheck my daddy never got
taxes none of them could afford. stevie's on
tonight and if you are lucky enough
to afford the ticket, you might even catch
the way stevie's mouth twitches for the old boys
on the block who might catch the concert
two decades later on a tv in the back room
of an oakland apartment. if it was not a dog
eat dog world, maybe my uncle's bones would
be thick enough to walk to the grocery store

all the way on the other side of town. instead,
the hospital chair sticks to my thighs, rips off
hairs when i stand to check on daddy, three hours
in and each arm is strapped down, milkshake
in and out, eyes in and out. i'm sure he is
thinking of belle isle chili hot dogs and watching
canada across the water, coast guard ships passing.
daring to dive. later, i will get daddy in the car and
drive slow, avoid campus police, highway patrol,
scrubs and smiles. daddy will want white castle burgers
for dinner and i will not remind him that this is california.
i will find a new west coast shake shack on the way home
and look around to make sure no one is watching. daddy
will get a milkshake, chocolate, and i will watch the machine
whir, blend, think of the blood sucked back into his veins
the scent of hospital soap. i will remember my girlfriend
telling me not to mark organ donor on my driver's license
or they will not bother saving me. blue blood. daddy's
pressure so high they won't let us leave the hospital,
won't let him sip on stories of a deserted detroit.
the doctors don't understand he hasn't slept in a week
he wants to go home, wants to remind himself he has
a bed, streetlamps, a daughter to tuck him in and
wait until the snores start. my friend's mother died
in this same hospital of the same cancer that found
my uncle's cells first, crept up my great-aunt and made
her sag into a small woman. a cancer they call black
so there is no study, no clinical trial, no other option
besides a miracle too small to detect in this cloud box
building where the only miracle is a nurse asking if
you want orange juice or lemonade, a milkshake
machine for your blood, making it out before dark.
before you realize streetlamps are not the only things
that make it difficult to find where you will sleep tonight
to sleep tonight at all.

Wet Nurse

suckle at a dry nipple
the color of
tear wet wood
there are bodies still
shielding the child

in a dry room
the child's favorite horses
banging on the door
saying supper isn't ready
it's always time to feed

the child grows
she coughs and stuffs
away into a hidden place
stays there, dreaming
until she hears
her cousins laughing
to wake the girl

the room remains
blue rags, sweat
everything still
lips moving
a knock on the door
pale children back
to find their mother

the child has
one soft mother
one stiff mother
crack open her
hands, golden like
the sun shines out

too many mothers
one vengeful
one humble
skull strong on milk
a child knows
the tit it fed from

the child is sure
her mother has
six hands
worth believing
for God
one mother pleads
for a whole lifetime
here is half

the child wants
a soft place to sleep
and a fable
one mother cries
for regret
for her child
God sings
a holy room's song

my great-grandmother's hand in the back pocket of all your jeans

Back when there was nothing but
plantations of blue, calluses yellowed
into a mountain peak on our palms

Back when this country was a windowless room
if not for our hips
when we created each side of the glass too

There was blue too much a galaxy to be called the color
of a child's winter lips
too purple to be seen in the back of a throat

Before they found an artificial way to color
we stood in front of a white white wall
and were the mural
they saw no picture in

You wouldn't know it but your favorite
pair of denim would not exist without
the stitch in my great-grandmother's left side

You would be nothing but a naked corpse
if not for a field spotted as her x-ray

How come we remember nothing more than corn and cotton?
How come we are always what we wear and not what has been worn?

To you, a tongue with all the taste buds burnt off is merely a muscle
To us, it is a marvel

All blood runs blue, runs out
After they mined something almost as glorious
as what they bent us over just to tend and harvest

After they tore down the crops and taught our fingers
how to crack and bleed a chalk white

we named our children the only true thing we had ever known: Indigo.
and you slipped on a new pair of jeans and never knew the difference.

Elegy for a body that once called itself mine

They say all things are meant to be. Except for you.
You were a breath meant to stay inside my body

Sweet thing, if only you knew how I mourn
for all the bliss you'll never know
All the clogged drains you were convinced
saved us from dark matter

I knew it the first time you tried to make a fist
and all your fingernails broke off in your palm

If it is meant to grow, I will water it
If it is meant to die, I will bury it.

If you had a name, I'd carve a headstone from my lost bones
But the worst kinds of pain are past naming

Sometimes I think of pinching the skin
wrinkling away from you like a baby elephant
like an aging grandmother
you always were caught in the sidewalk cracks of time

Before I could imagine existing without you,
I worshiped at the grave of your coin sized stomach

I wished you empty as if it was possible
for me to still be whole, living off nothing but a small girl's hope

I know what you would think of me now
swimming in your skeleton
Me and you, a tree's leaves and its trunk

you were always meant to fall

On Fried Chicken and Watermelon

The father of a daughter
who has seen too much
was once a boy
refusing anything but cap'n crunch
cereal dry and stuffed into every socket of his muscled abdomen
teenage boys walking down a deadened street
strung together in crumbs

> Shame is a highway with no end or beginning
> are you first or last in line? have you been here
> forever or has it only just begun

The father of the daughter
who is perpetually scared
forgets to eat for twenty hours a day
and the daughter lies to her doctor and says
she sleeps nine hours every night
these lengths they go to
to escape their stomachs
Father and daughter stuck at sixteen
in the same revolving decades
shoving fried gizzards in their mouths
just to chew and spit them back out

> They love to eat. The whole family pretends this isn't true
> because who are they
> to be exactly what this country expects, to sustain
> themselves with the cheapest hunk of meat from the grocery store
> to be ravenous, insatiable, unfinished

The grandmother of the father of the daughter
who laughs like a hiccuping child

makes oxtail stew every time a cloud appears
and doesn't bother blowing
on the spoon before it touches her gums.
the daughter stares at her lunch
a pb&j she never ate as a child,
oil coming out of her nose pores
mouth burning from jerk rub.
tonight her body is a reckoning.

      The father of the whiplashed daughter
      has decided not to deprive them
      the juice dripping from a robust thigh tonight

      they devour okra
          and goat
          and greens
          and grilled peaches
          and jambalaya
          and every last bit of anything
      they can get their hands on
      they make divine out of scraps
      they make babies out of torment

The daughter of the father
who will never know satisfaction
goes to bed full every night now,
unafraid of the extra pounds
hanging from her upper arms; she calls this
inherited flesh. she calls this luxury stretchings.

The father of the daughter
who is finally just right
remembers cap'n crunch and nothing else
until she feeds him dutch apple pie / ham / stew
and he is a little boy again

bloated with hope,
he is in the backseat exiting the highway
his grandmother driving while she sips on sweet tea
and for the first time all century,
none of them
are hungry

My greatest-grandmother's will

This poem is an erasure of the last will and testament of Nan Payne's enslaver.

In the name of   state

          of body   memory and knowing

          now   being one   on the

   Wateree river   of three hundred

        Negroes   called   Nan,

    horses and cattle and   life.

I give   my   youngest boy   one

      will   and the   negroes

shall   descend.   the

lawful heirs of   my body   not to be sold   away.

            one plantation   one hundred acres

      bounding

        myself

        my daughter   one Negro woman called

one Negroe girl called

I   Rose with

                                wine, it is

my will that one

child

      die

    that   so losing shall   entitle

                         one of my

Children   to   forever. I give unto my beloved girl

    this   last   day of   one Thousand Seven hundred and

Ninety.

Under the Tongue

When you grow up, you will forget it all. And isn't that a solace?
the last forty years
dandelion fluff blown away   one day translucent
                                    the next, gone.

Forgetting is in our bones, black as wood rot
Forgetting is in the splinters you let absorb beyond sight
from all those hardwood floors we didn't sand

Blueberries
A crossword puzzle
One glass of red wine before bed

A wives' tale about chewing bark
Counting the number of steps from your bedside table
to the toilet

Live
while you still can
fill your mouth with holy ghosts
        make it edible.
        make it smooth.

Memory is halfway to dying the moment it is made.
You are still young. Your silver hairs only touch the middle of your earlobes.

There is still time
to forget
you are trying to remember.

womanhood

wash day

on the days i find myself too swollen to fit inside the bathtub, i wash myself in the backyard / a teapot of water hot enuf to burn / i've been told all my life to stop being so gotdamn dirty. dirty as in loud. i shave my legs on the pavement / i shave my pussy upside down standing on my head in the middle of the street. my shower takes so long i lose hot water trying to unknot hair i once thought wasn't worth taming in the first place. i pee after i fuck / i water the plants after i fuck cause i like to give back. in high school i couldn't find a way to sneak out of the house so i walked out the front door / every door is mine now and i hose myself down in the driveway until all the chalk has run into a blur / and i am still so / gotdamn / dirty

going in

my girlhood grown
a superbloom of dread

once there was
a small girl pining
now there is
a righteous fist

cooped up in a
man's best nightmare
i taught myself
the purple blaze
of my name
spoken soft

looking out at
a decade of
resuscitated hearts
i clad copper armor
ready for my
inherited heartbreak

instead i found
a strawberry moon
my girlhood grown
a parallel peak

how to love a woman sailing the sky

the only thing that
surprised me more than
all the oceans soaked
in salt was the day
after all my chasing
all your running
you stopped
twirled around
and touched your fingertips
to the crescent of my
collarbone

i have been a woman
sailing the sky
i have been a girl
clung tight to the branches
i have been a daughter
splayed out on a boat
of ice

and then I was Yours.

i was born to floating people
who drank from the clouds
that held them until there
was nothing but blue and
one spectacular drop

i searched for something solid
so long i forgot my body itself
was not made of mist or malice
you reached out your hand

i flinched
until you showed me you
were not reaching through me
but for me

and then I was Yours.

strip

on the pole i'm so woman i've got a callused tongue and hips so rough i make all the women who have loved me swoon. they ask if i'm a stripper and i say what if i am. what if drinking syrup straight from the bottle don't make you sticky. make me auntie's baby. aunt jemima carved from manifest destiny and laid out to dry as she nursed a white girl's newborn baby. jemima would have killed for this body roll. for booty shorts and titties bouncing free. we sweat. we shimmy. we let our thighs cottage cheese jiggle and don't pay no mind. if i gave a shit about respectability politics, i would be sweet but not sexy. a child is holy but far from the jungle of her conception. never sex. always spit. i spin around my pole and taste metal, so easily mistaken for blood and salt and all things gaping. when i dance i am young and forgetful, freshly birthed from wombs and women i don't have to think about beyond the flesh today. what if the mammy was naked but not a jezebel? what if we did not need a name for skin? it is not a colorblind sentiment, it is a child who wants to steal a cookie and eat it warm. it is simple, knotted as my hair when i don't wear my bonnet because last night was steamy and free and i can't be bothered. it is wicked.

Waterfalling

the first mistake anyone made was telling
children love was a prerequisite to skin
or maybe that skin was a prerequisite
to a lifetime of sloppy goodbyes

i didn't know it
but there was good buried
in the landmines of all this wanting
and i struck it
in the moment she pulls out a candle for every birthday
she wasn't there to celebrate
i unearthed it
in the quiet buzz of her eyes
waterfalling down her cheeks
every time i read to her
even when it is not my story

If biology could explain it all
we would never know of fairies or prayers
and wouldn't it be a shame to not kneel at her feet
and hum her dreams of
us, intertwined, creating?

i didn't know it
but there is a gift hiding
in the grief of what our
bodies cannot do on their own

we choose
we chase
we love without
all the terror of accidents
because this dream is ours
and it is wistful
it is wise
it is a wonder

i didn't know it but
in all the misconceptions of heartbeats and
loose tongues, the most dangerous
is that you cannot have all of this
without its oppositional force

They say you cannot truly appreciate summer
without the winter before
but i am sprung up from a California drought
and i open my mouth, tilt my chin
to sky and taste every last ray
radiant as her heart
backlit by the light
of all those birthday candles
And it is still golden.
And she is still mine.

what to do when you see a Black woman cry

stop. hum a little / just for some sound / just for a way to fill us up
it is streetlamp time / all moon-cheeked black girls are
mourning / a wailing kind of undoing
don't mistake this as a tragedy / it is sacred
don't mistake this as a glorious pain / we hurt.

don't tell me it will be alright.
make me a gourmet meal and don't expect me
to do the dishes after
don't try to hug me without asking first
if i slept last night / if i need some
jasmine tea / and a bath in a tub
deep enough to fit my grief

and if i say i want a hug
don't touch my hair while you do it / don't twist
my braids around your fingers
or tell me my fro is matted in the back
from banging my head
on the wall of so many askings

you think we are sobbing for the men,
but we are praying for the men / their favorite
sweat-soaked t-shirts
we are screeching for our thighs
for our throats / and our teeth-chipping / for the terror
and the ceremony / and the unending always
of this sky

so if i let you see a tear drip / if i let you see my teeth chatter
know you are witnessing a miracle
know you are not entitled to my face crack / head shake / sob
but i do not cry in front of just anyone
so stop. hum a little / just for some sound / just to fill me up

Respect

I leave the house without my edges laid
a bonnet disguised in nothing but black sheen
a dress that refuses to hide my bounce
open-toed shoes I will bang on the edge of a curb as I run from
                   something. always something.

tell me you are afraid of my gait without ever acknowledging I have walked here

     a chorus of voices in a meeting where I am the topic of discussion
     and nowhere do I hear the whistle of wind between my gap teeth

     a boys' huddle of numbers as we pass, one after the other
     3, 7, 5, 10.
     the only spectrum I have wanted to exist nowhere and everywhere at once

Aretha said R.E.S.P.E.C.T.
     and I know you know how to spell
     I know you know how to consume
     always have, since the first time you sought out
     a body only to carve it of its throat

     yet when Aretha erupts from the speaker in the background of
                      a street

                                    office

                          bar

          it is as though she sang a babble of sounds
           and you, belting along, heard nothing but your own tapping feet

I am sixteen in a club I should not be in
5'3" swollen cheeked, glossy eyed
    the bouncer grabs at my ass
    the sweat crawls at my gel and undoes it into widow's peak
    I am wearing the same thing I wore to junior chemistry today
    what a warped world that believes me
    only when I say what you want to hear

One day, when I strut into the meeting in a silk scarf
the same shade as my busted open toe
when I turn around and chase you back down the street
at the first sign of a whistle
when I go on the hunt for anyone who considered
me not worthy of more than a wink and a spilled shot
a round of applause and a raised glass
who considered me
        not a regal mess of a woman,
        a vicious gospel of a voice,
        a shrine of a long-passed miracle
        you are lucky enough to witness revived

when it is all over
you will wish you had seen more than my lips in motion
you will wish you had heard more than the buzz
of your adam's apple at the sight of my dress

and by the time I am holy enough
you cower at my demand of a little
R.E.S.P.E.C.T.
we both will know
it is too little
too late

After Want by Joan Larkin

I want a three bedroom house and a child
out of each of our eggs
She wants this apartment
and both my hands to hold, maybe one day
a bathtub to soak in
I want to buy every book I lay my eyes on
and stack them like a border between us
      and everything
She wants a bookshelf made of solid white oak
and a library card to fill it with
      then empty it again at the end of the month

I want ten vacations and endless
ocean blue, my summer foundation in the winter
She wants to stay put,
light up a gas fireplace, take a nap
on the stretches of my stomach
I want to work into the night
until I remember I have not kissed her today
She wants to come home
from the office and wrap herself around me before sunset
I want two cars, a bungalow
with an in law unit and a hose, a red pit bull
the color of her hair in the sun, two babies named
after all the women I have been, a pool to dive in,
a moon to sip, an airport that takes us
to everywhere at once. Her. always Her.

She wants to no longer want anything at all
lock the door at night and
hope for nothing; I want a diamond ring

without the diamond, meaning I want
her hair knotted on my finger
I want to dream up forever
She wants a forever
of right nows
I look at her
She looks back
and I have never
wanted anything
more

For the Women I Twerk To

Before we bounce we body roll
pay our respects to you
tongue out, wet and bumpy
like the drive to Hollywood
in a stolen station wagon
To you, for letting this ass
blubber and bitch and eat up
all the air particles too dirty for a rhyme
this clean
sassy moody nasty
Tonight the lights so low
we can't tell if that's sweat or blood
or discharge
Pussy like water
overflowing in the studio
bass hopped to the side
My grandmother would have had a stroke
to see us this free tonight
Can you go upside down
and still shake
ring around the rosie and drop it low
How bout a trip to the strip
we tip better than any suit
hide bills in thick thighs, thick waists
Fuck an orgy
we yadayadayada screech and twist
our ankles til it ripple up the thighs
more cellulite, more shimmy
Fuck all your free time
we got a schedule
strict, hour to hour, don't be late

slap that ass and kiss it better
I'm my own lover tonight
I wipe myself down in a
ripped bandana and thank God
Thank you very much

Futurist

My brother wants two babies and a house in a *good* neighborhood
A wife with five pairs of shoes and the sense to not stick a knife in the toaster

I want my own hill. The house can come afterward, first I want somewhere
to tumble. Somewhere a fire will have to climb before it singes my baby's fresh curls

Me and my woman got screaming wombs. Baby fever all up inside my eardrums
It is a human urge, to multiply, to subject a child to all your sanded wanting

If god is my great-grandmother's palm lines, I am praying through the stained glass window
through refracting light. Give my daddy a second chance, a grandbaby with my eclipsed eyes

Tell me how to birth a child into death zone, how to feed her colostrum mixed
in smoke from our backyard. We'll build a bunker into the hillside for a chance

at a legacy. At least my brother can call his wanting an accident. At least my daddy
will see the grave before he sees his cd collection drowned in toxified water

Cotton don't grow here no more. Sweet potatoes don't either. No yams to mash up
and feed to infant still pushing teeth through soft gum. Mama wants you to live

on infertile ground. Lights out. Generational wealth gold in California's mined hills.
Cousins meet in the bunker, hands pressed to hearts thumping like granddaddy's off beat bass.

poem for reckoning day

I resurrect the Big House
32 miles from memphis
resurrect it from clay soil
wet with flashbacks
and revelations
I greet the door with
the ball of my foot
leathered from the mecca
it took three lifetimes
to complete
waltz up the stairs
to the room my women
yawned and yellowed
scrape hands across the
walls and tattoo myself
in splinters
looking for words
where there will be no writing
no names
only the knocks of centuries
spent flooding
flickering
forfeiting
our top layer of skin
in the name of bearings
I see red in the floorboards
and believe it
my fourth great-grandmother's
my great-grandmother's
mine
sunken and seeped where wood
goes to die, where bleach goes

to apologize for the wounds
we cannot manufacture
or erase
I resurrect the Big House
with this family's gun held to
the temple of its sin
and prepare to shoot
we don't talk about how
we crack in the night
my pillowcase a mortuary
my eye mask a renaissance
of weeping
we don't talk about
our third eye, our fourth ear
the beasts we become to
rebel
like we don't talk about
where the green eyes
come from
until I kneel on the grave
of a tennessee timeline
and release every finger in all
my grandmothers' fists
I resurrect the Big House
cover it in gasoline
and burn it down
set fire to this corner of
tennessee like it will
turn every other house
our women's hips have
been split open in to flames
like it will fill all the gaps
in my bloodline
where men made
an ocean of our bodies

waiting and ready to swallow
when I resurrect the Big House,
I will resurrect every doorway
that has turned my family tree
into a battleground
made fences into weapons
a house hides every gash
a house shelters every
bull's insistent stampedes
into our chests
i find a stone in every city
every lake
we have attempted to make
into sanctuary
line them along my windowsill
light splits them open into shards
of my grandmothers' eyes
we stare into each other
resurrect each other
like breath
like ghost woman full
hold hands as we walk
into the root of it
where the mauling of our
bodies became tradition
resurrect tennessee
burn
resurrect backlit porches
burn
resurrect crescent scars, bite marks
burn
until we are fire women
because we are fire women
plantation to nashville to detroit to oakland
we simmer

acknowledgments

Thank you to the generations of poets, particularly the black women before me, who have nurtured, charged, and stirred me awake. All the love and gratitude to Cece Jordan for your kind and thoughtful eyes; I'm endlessly thankful to have grown as a poet under your mentorship. To my editors, Diana Miller and Deb Garrison, and my agents, Lucy Carson and Molly Friedrich, for patiently watching this collection evolve with me. To Michael Morris, for being the cover designer of my dreams and always conjuring the perfect image to fit all these words. To Mo, for being the heart of all my love poems and for crying almost every time you read a new one so I'd know if it was good. And, lastly, to my hood, in all definitions of the term, for giving me a world abundant in poetry.

A NOTE ON THE TYPE

This book was set in Chaparral, an Adobe original typeface designed by Carol
Twombly and released in 1997. Chaparral was the last typeface Twombly
designed before she left Adobe and perhaps retired from type design in 1999.

Composed by North Market Street Graphics, Lancaster, Pennsylvania
Printed and bound by Lakeside Book Company, Harrisonburg, Virginia
Designed by Maggie Hinders